Apples In Winter

Liam Aungier

DOGHOUSE

Apples In Winter
is published by
DOGHOUSE
P.O. Box 312
Tralee G.P.O.
Co. Kerry
Ireland
TEL: +353 (0)66 7137547   email: doghouse312@eircom.net
www.doghousebooks.ie
Copyright : Liam Aungier, September, 2005

ISBN 0-9546487-8-1

Edited for DOGHOUSE by Noel King

Cover illustration: Alice King Mullkeen

Printed by Tralee Printing Works, Denny Street, Tralee

Further copies available at 12 euro, post free, from the above address,
cheques etc. payable to DOGHOUSE.

Doghouse is a non-profit taking company, aiming to publish the best of liter-
ary works by Irish born writers. Donations are welcome and will be acknowl-
edged on this page.

For our 2005 publications, heartfelt thanks for donations to:

Tuatha Chiarraí   **Independent News & Media PLC**
Pauline Bewick; Bus Eireann; CH Chemists; Cill Rialaig Project; Tom Coffey;
Dr. Donal Daly; Dr. Pat English; ESB Networks; Gallagher's (Ireland) Ltd;
Mrs Norrie Gentleman; William H. Giles & Co.; Hi Notes Music Co.;
Donal Kelliher, Solicitor; Kelliher's Hardware; Kelliher's Property Holding Co.;
Kingdom Restaurants; Liscahane Nurseries; Philip J. Manzor & Co.; Murphy,
Ramsay, Walsh, Solicitors; Florrie O'Carroll; Mr.Patrick J.F. O'Sullivan;
Pierce & Fitzgibbon, Solicitors, Mr. Paddy Prendergast; Stockbyte.

for my parents
Anne and William Aungier

Acknowledgments are due to editors of the following where these poems or versions of them were first published:

Books Ireland; The Burning Bush; Imagine; The Irish Times; Poetry Ireland Review; The Poetry Mill; Reality; Riposte; Slacker (UK); Southword; The Stinging Fly; The Stony Thursday Book; Stroan; Siglamag;
The Waterford Review; Writing in the West (The Connacht Tribune); Under Brigid's Cloak (anthology of Kildare writers); Wildeside.

Aphrodite in the Gallery – 1st place Coothill Poetry Competition, 1994

Paul Baumer, 1913 – Ist place The South Tipperary Poetry Competition, 1994

Snapshot – 2nd Edgeworthstown Literary Awards, 1997

A version of this manuscript took 2nd place in the 1998 and in the 1999 Patrick Kavanagh Award

Thanks also to Noel King, Editor, DOGHOUSE books

Contents

Snapshot, Sept 1st 1939

A hawk soars upside-down beneath my meadows,
trees plunge into the depths of sky.
In this free moment before lunch
I shiver on a wind-chilled hill behind the farm
with a box-camera, its viewfinder inverting
the patchwork fields, the scudding clouds.

I aim – the shutter snaps behind the lens –
then wind the film on and stroll towards home,
finding that in the sun-filled kitchen
saucepans boil over, a kettle steams unnoticed.
In the polished darkness of the parlour
my sisters surround the wireless
stuttering the headline news
turning the world upside-down forever.

History Lesson

The obscure gleam of medieval gold; lustre
of silver pennies. The County Museum
Middle Ages Room; twenty teenage students jostle
amongst a hoard of puzzle jugs, their teacher
tells them of the ancient town and they feign interest
in trade routes, guilds and murage.
But what they truly want is to be out
in the market town amongst the makeshift stalls
and narrow lanes, haggling for sweet-meats
in the antique square, the cobbled streets
ringing with the song of their silver florins.

Aubade

I wouldn't hear you wake.
Fearing to wake me
you'd slip from between our sheets,
dress in the dark and
with your shoes in your hand,
creak open the door.
Sometimes I'd wake
hearing the hall door shut.
Still hours to lectures,
I'd turn beneath the blankets
onto your side,
lie in the warmth your body left.

Geography

Sumatra, Ceylon, St. Petersburg
on the flattened Earth, pinned
to the classroom wall above his desk.

My great-uncle is telling of his boyhood
how each slow April afternoon
a pale sun crinkled the fading map.

Deaf to history's lesson,
he day-dreamed of palaces and pagodas,
his tongue lisping the names of

Sudan, Zanzibar, Dar es Salaam,
none of which he would ever see.
The place-names of his world

would interest few cartographers:
Killmeague, Lowtown, Ballyteague,
Messines, Frezenberg, Passchendale.

In My Father's House Are Many Rooms

The priest's words at the graveside
are scattered by November wind
as the casket is lowered

clay thuds on its lid, and the women break
into a last sorrowful mystery;
while high above our heads, an aircraft
– its silver wings flashing in the chill light –
flies to the New World.

Small World

The London rush-hour
was ringing in his ear
– Caroline's sister in England
had phoned out of the blue –
Jason, our youngest
in the hallway
in the darkening hush
of an Irish evening,
hearing for the first time
the bustle of Piccadilly,
snarl of traffic,
muffled thunder
of a passing bus.
I take the receiver
and he shuffles back
into the still
bird-echoing fields
of a suddenly smaller world.

The ESB Man

Dark as thought, this power house
of turbines and pressure-gauges, where nightly
my father burned the raw fuel of experience
to insubstantial force,
and by these unseeing labours brought
to our darkest moments
this lyrical and apprehending light.

In War Time

for my father, William Aungier

That autumn the wireless stuttered
with the names of foreign battles,
news of Paulus' *inexorable triumph,*
Russia's defiance,
soup freezing in front-line kitchens,
bombs showering backstreets of London,
while the travelling cinemas flashed
home to every Irish village
the moonscape of Stalingrad.

At thirteen, your fingers numbed by frost,
you spent days snagging turnips,
while at night in your oil-lit bedroom,
your hands tuned a Russian plywood fiddle;
bombarded the silence with a slow air.

Dreaming of China

...and sorrow, sorrow like rain... – Li Po

The moon fills the window where I sit.
Far from Chang-an, an Irish evening trickles down,
exiles the leafless willows from my sight. Only
your words for company: *Lament of the Frontier Guard*,
its yellowed leaves exhale the scent of grief,
the loneliness of desolate fields.
Clouds disguise the moon.
Invisible trees stagger in the dark.
Drunk on your words, I dream
of your forgotten village,
two continents and a thousand years away –
the rain falling on its uncut grass.

village ennui

evening settles in
        shadows
creep across the uncut lawn
        already
the day's post has been collected
        the tabloid papers lie
unsold in the village shop
        a stray
dog sleeps curled in its doorway
        in an hour
the street-lights will start
banishing what hope we had of stars

Photograph of a Refugee

The light of Germany was fading.
Snapped in the gloom of exodus
you lean over the ship's rail:
the grey land of your childhood
flows out of focus;
your mother's house,
the smell of coal smoke in November streets,
those nights you spent surveying the fixed stars
dreaming of Ingrid;
memories bound for a New World.

A blurred seagull hangs motionless
above your ship, as the lights
of Lübeck drown in the monochrome,
the only star this night the yellow star
pinned against your heart.

Moment Musicale

In the dark silence of the hall a piano weeps;
hunched over the keyboard a frail Chinese
is playing Chopin, the ivory keys
sob under his fingertips. Isaac sits
in a stream of melody as autumn rain
drums on the starless windows.
In another land, another evening,

drizzle darkened a Sunday afternoon.
He stood at a window, raindrops blurring
the street, from the next room a piano:
Ingrid, her head nodding over the yellowing keys,
filled the evening with a melancholy waltz,
the last chord fading to the rain's applause.

First Born

He was safe in the throbbing cave,
curled in its concave shell, his ears
accustomed to its tides of blood,
his eyes not curious for the light

before they reached him, fished him out
head first, our catch, our exile
who screams at us now with all
his fury as we weep with joy.

You Never Can Tell

Widow, mother of six and old
as Methuselah, we altar boys
would see her every Sunday
at early mass, kneeling
in the front row, summer or winter
wearing the one black coat. So
when Fr. Grogan sermonized
on *the evils of foreign ways,* we smiled,
pitying the woman we thought she was:
naive, brow-beaten, over-awed,
but tucked safely under the kneeling-board
fresh, carefully folded, not yet read
– her *News of the World*.

Cowboy Pictures

A lone rider gallops across the prairie,
the Union Stage is twenty minutes late
in Lyons' Travelling Cinema, pitched
– for one week only – in Ryan's field.
The local boys light Woodbines in the back row,
blue smoke spirals in a shaft of light
as Randolph Scott - a tin star on his lapel -
loads a revolver, gathers up a posse.

Later, under a canopy of stars they'll ride
across the prairies of Roscommon,
moonlight reducing the landscape to monochrome,
turning villages into one-horse towns,
Brennan's sheepdog is a lost coyote
as farm house chimneys blow
smoke signals to a silver dollar moon.

Preludes

Had we arrived too early? Alone
we sat in the cathedral's silence,
you were thumbing your program
promising: J.S.Bach - *Chorale
Preludes*. Remember?
First week of our engagement,
your cotton dress
thin to the cathedral's chill
and I draped my jacket
around your shoulders;
the tiled floor
was sprinkled with confetti,
a poster on the notice board
offered marriage guidance,
and a lone candle
on the lady altar
petering out.
Outside the unexpected
storm rehearsed its fury.

Above My Head Granite Angels Soar

Guidebook in hand, I imagine
five hundred years ago
and the half-completed church
a forest of scaffolding...

...the wooden gantry
glowed in the evening light
to the plainchant of chisels...

...masons and journeymen,
their calloused hands
numbed by November cold,
released seraphs
from the rough uneven stone...

...basalt columns foliate
in the dappled nave,
limestone blooms.

Seeing Atlantis

We were standing in the midnight garden,
Mark and I, heads turned skywards
our eyes smarting under the cold stars
for this vision of shuttle *Atlantis* –
a splinter of light, drifting
through the shimmering dark,
sketching an arc across the northern sky.

We believed we had witnessed
something miraculous, but they

miles above us in their weightless drift
had witnessed something more:

our tiny world, its blue and white
like a flawed sapphire swimming in the velvet dark
with all the hopes and fears it held that night.

Stone

A stone-age knife,
half smooth as a pearl,
half razor sharp.
I lift it – notice
its heaviness, it holds
the weight of centuries.

Shaped before Buddha,
before John preached
in the wilderness,
you might mistake it
for Cain's murder weapon.

I try its cruel edge
with my thumb, note
how exactly it fits
in the hollow of my hand.

Paul Baumer, 1913

Saturday evening in the Baumers' terraced home,
the domestic routine, the smell
of potato-cakes from your mother's
cramped and steamy kitchen, your father
gaunt and weary on the landing, home from work,
brushing his only suit for tomorrow's Mass –
their banal and happy lives; a quiet heroism
no history will record. And you, Paul,
wombed in this flood of the familiar, studying
for school the glories of the Seven Years' War,
besieged by Heine, Goethe, Schiller,
arrayed on makeshift bookshelves;
the centuries of culture which will not save you
from the approaching slaughter. A rattle
of delph. Your mother calls *Supper*
and the Angelus tolls down the darkening street.

Alexandria

He saw you only once. Sailing to Tyre
he was on deck, off-duty, he remembers,
a light breeze ruffled his thinning hair.
He squinted against the sun to see
the embrace of your harbour, the silent cranes
loading and unloading; imagined
wharf-side taverns, narrow shaded lanes,
the tossed sheets of some illicit bed.

Imagined too that you should meet again.
But his life would be spent out in other towns,
small towns, nondescript and miles inshore,
their terraced houses overlooked by spires.
He stayed on deck for a long time that day,
watching the great city slip from his grasp.

Brownie Six-20

Brown fields, brown hills, brown sky,
brown roses flowering against a brown wall:
my mother's photographs. In the dark
of a winter's afternoon, my eyes
are squinting to decipher people
lost in the grain of this vanished world;
faces I cannot name returning my gaze,

and Mum, at half my age
her Brownie Six-20
capturing the fleeting clouds, roses
jostling in the sunlight, red and green,
filling the viewfinder with transient joy.

Caroline with Guitar

She is enraptured, my wife,
her head inclined over the humming strings,
her small hand curved about its neck.
Their music fills our house.
                    I spy her
reflection in the bedroom mirror
and I might play the jealous husband,
the foolish cuckold, did I not trust
that tonight, this instrument put
away   we will improvise
our own intimate recital.

The Death of Edgar Degas

A final evening. In your semi-conscious room
a silhouette unlocks a case of scalpels,
then shakes his head. Blind as Homer,
your mind, jumbled with dancers and bronze horses,
drifts beyond these curtained windows. Outside
it is a usual September: leaves blush
to the expected shade of red, the evening tram
jangles down the boulevard on schedule,
as the public clocks chime out your dying hours.
Again the doctor searches for your pulse, tomorrow
papers will announce your funeral arrangements.

The Inheritors

I

They forged a path – Sunday after Sunday –
walking across the commons to their church:
on winter mornings their boots
crushed the sparkling snowfall, in spring
the newly-flowered buttercups, until
the grass withered and the earth
turned hard as the commandments of their faith.

II

And now their names are remembered
only on the lichened stones
angled in the abandoned church-yard
where once they walked, wild clovers
proliferate, the meadow-sweets
increase and multiply, and a field mouse
scuttles through the dew-soaked undergrowth,
inheriting the earth.

Good Friday Stations

An altar boy worries
over a guttering candle.

At about the ninth hour
the young curate beseeches us all:

publicans and tax collectors,
scribes and sinners,

to be born again. We nod
our grey heads in agreement.

A seven-month-old child,
her blonde head pillowed

on her father's shoulder,
slumbers,

her tiny fist clenched
in the innocence of sleep.

Saints glow in the gothic windows,
behind each hallowed head

the raised Eucharist of the sun
is judging the world,

dividing Creation
into light and shade.

Hephaistos

Hephaistos, the renowned smith – The Iliad

A man of few words and little grace,
Peter Carey, bachelor, pensioner,
village farrier. As a child
I'd see him Sunday mornings
awkward in an ill-fitting suit,
hobbling home from early Mass.
And when I was eight or nine he died.

So imagine my surprise to meet him now,
this afternoon in the college library,
to find him translated
between the covers of the *Iliad,*
conversing with the Immortals;
deity of the dragging footsteps,
old artificer, fire-god.

Galatea in Marble

For centuries I slumbered in the stone.
Outside
an ice-age rose and fell,
a forest soared, and then
the clamour of axes,

none of which concerned me.
Until he found me:
the mortal
who made me what I am

in his dusty, cluttered workshop;
how he laboured
for the first kiss
of sunlight on my shoulders,
my pale reflection swimming in his eyes.

Aphrodite in the Gallery

I

Reposed and shaded in the trembling heat,
Aphrodite slumbers on the grass
and at her outstretched feet husks of fruit
and emptied casks of wine recall
the Dionysian feast whose revellers
– these nymphs and satyrs – dream or lie in love
beneath the towering pine in whose high branch
a nightingale heralds the evening star
and further off upon the Tuscan hills
two oxen are ploughing the painted fields;
from a peasant's ivied home a trail of smoke
drifts and dissolves into the indigo sky.

II

I stagger back amazed and later on
the long drive to the loveless suburbs
dreaming of such calm, such opulent repose.
The dead click of the latch-key resounds
through the empty flat,
evening collapses to the roar of traffic,
the klaxon birdsong of police cars,
until suddenly looming out of the gloom
that baroque pastorale – its absurd joy
a brief respite from the trembling heat,
– a little star to set against the night.

Honey in December

for Peter Connolly

Through the dazzling cold of a December dawn
you make this winter's journey – drive
past songless woods and the dead fields, leaving
your farmhouse and from its bee hives bring
to my invalid and ageing father
your unageing friendship
and a gift of honey.

Pale as frost in the kitchen's electric heat,
my father revives in your shared talk
above the emptied tea-cups, and the honey jar
half empty of its amber, your words
recalling the summer of his days as the sticky
sweetened juice awakes the memory
of sunlight in the flowering hedges
– in a winter's vapid chill the taste of summer.

Spring Wedding

Through the veil of raindrops on the kitchen window
you watch your husband trudge back from ploughing;
my jacket soaked, my boots sucking
through farm-yard mud, but behind me
the ground swells with life,
tilled fields are nourished by this downpour,
ash trees heavy with leaf-buds,
green hedges dripping in the blue rain.

This day twelve months ago you stood
in the white sunlight of the village church
vowing for better or worse. You remember
the altar decked with flowers
your gleaming dress. You smile to think
you'd never fit it now: each morning
in the wardrobe mirror your reflection blossoms
as each slow day the life within you grows.

Neolithic

A language carved in stone:
chevrons and spirals,
ovals, lozenges.
I had not hoped
for such a hoard as this
in a house of the dead
hollowed under a hill,
an iconography I can see
but cannot read. My guide,
crouching beside me
in this womb of rock,
tells how these motifs
are found all about
our island. I want to ask
if he might decipher
these signs the ancients
left us, but I know
no-one
of our generation can.
And then we turn,
begin our long back-crawl
through the twisting,
stone-lined passage
towards the light,
our shadows trailing us like afterbirth,
our eyes dazzled by the ancient sun.

Two Brothers

His cattle stumble through the morning's frost,
their foul breaths steaming, their shit
slapping the narrow road before him.

Eamonn, left at home to labour on the farm,
drives them on from milking and envies
his brother in America;

Seamus, made good,
seller of second-hand autos,

who sleeps now
in the small hours of Albany,

dreaming of far off hills, cattle drowsing
in the sweet grass of morning.

The Aqueduct

Call it a miracle; the only landmark in
an unmarked landscape – a stone bridge bearing
the waters of the Grand Canal
above a limpid stream.
                    Once,
surprised by the passion of a summer storm
we sheltered there. I remember
the sky's furious cascade and how
we crouched together under the arch,
so close I could feel your breath
warm against my face.
                    Afterwards
the earth smelt of rain.
You held my arm as we side-stepped
from under our limestone roof,
into a quiet and glistening world.

A Vermeer Woman

She stood before the window
smocked in sunlight,
her white-stained hands moulding
flour, butter, buttermilk,
into a tender paste.
Half an hour later
her house was nourished
by the smell of baking.
When the clock chimed
half-past-three
the oven was opened,
bicycles rattled outside –
her children returned from school.
She handed out tea and buttered slices,
still warm tokens of affection,
the oil-cloth littered
with crumbs of love.

Last Meeting

The very dead of winter.
Fields shrouded in snow,
a sliver of moon
caught in a frozen sky
and the countryside silent as a grave.

But we were safe
in your gleaming kitchen,
my hands cupping a mug
of coffee
as you told me –

Then I awoke.
A summer's morning:
cacophony of birdsong
and the curtained window
glowing in the dawn.

Valediction

Half-way between
one age and another
my hands rummaged
in boxes cobwebbed with age,
excavating childhood detritus;
a papier-maché army
defeated at last
by dampness and neglect.
The bonfire awaits,
memories, dust, ashes
and these words.

A German War Requiem

Three fishermen found you
tangled in their nets off Donegal,
your hair knotted with seaweed,
a kriegsmarine uniform covering
your body stiff as coral.
Hauled aboard the trawler
onto a bier of wriggling catch,
a seagull picked at your one remaining eye,
fought off by the cabin-boy who saw you
as a conscript to an evil cause, but no enemy,
a victim tangled in a mesh of events,
drowned by history.

Hedgehog

Each night you trek our moonlit lawn,
nose sniffing the air, brown eyes
foraging in the dark for a dish
nestling in the wet grass, before
your muddied snout slobbers
over its feast of milksops.

Sitting together on the front porch step
we spy your progress. My father,
frail and convalescing,
whispers how he'd found you weeks before
weak and battle-wounded,

his pale hand points out the gloom,
the darkness rustles: meal ended
you retreat into the welcoming night,
old warrior, nursed by gentleness.

Letter from Seville

All day it had rained, rain
lashing Connacht Street,
running down the window where I sit
waiting for word of you, listening
to the downpipes gurgle,
tattoo of raindrops on the glass,
a symphony of weeping, but from you
only silence.

The weather slowly clears.
The evening post
brings an envelope from Spain,
its paper damp, postmark
blurred as if by tears.
I sit in the park reading
your words under the dripping elms,
thinking of you in the distant south
as puddled streets dry in the evening sun.

A Civil Service

Locked in the top drawer of his desk,
(the key of which is held by him alone),
he keeps a slim volume of Cavafy,
occasionally to be read, but mostly
it's enough just to know it's there
in the same dusty office as the ledgers:
a minor clerk who, when the time presents
itself, slips into its pages,

the way you might, of an afternoon
slip through the side-door of a church,
but not to pray or to be confessed,
in the centre of the city at last alone
to bathe a moment in its stillness, in
the vast, spinning world, this point of rest.

The Music Lesson

In the dark silence of her parlour I practice
scales and chords, my hands strained
to capture, between cadences and riffs,
life's incidental music.
Miss Lynch
flings open a window on a soundscape
more marvellous than I could guess at:

a lorry engine warbles in the heat;
women's voices;
somewhere a radio's notes
splash into the yawning street;
the mid-day train shudders across river,
sets the steel bridge ringing like a gamelan;
ending my lesson with its cadenza.

On First Hearing His Name

"Federico García Lorca," adeir an buachaill.
An east wind was singing its Cante Jondo
and a Gypsy sun was riding across the sky. I
was at the back, keeping my head down
in Irish Class, astounded to have heard
in the middle of our *Dúil*
the trochees and the dactyl of your name.

Later there would be lemon groves and guitars,
exotic fruits, the voice of your poems,
murmur of a fountain in a village square.
But for that moment I was pleased just
to feel in my mouth your Latinate music,
Federico, Federico García...

* Dúil: a collection of short stories by Liam O'Flaherty

* adeir an buachaill: said the boy

* Liam O'Flaherty: Oifig an Phoist (The Post Office)

New House

His footsteps echo through the empty rooms,
size fours dashing on the creaking stairs.
In the kitchen the builder's agent and I
quibble over terms. He stands
in a bright room. No furniture. White flowers
bloom on the wallpaper and outside
a little window: the quiet town,
the blinding heat of spring, three girls
playing hopscotch in the evening street
dancing over the chalked pavement.
He would like this room, he hears
the deep song of a passing car.
Downstairs the argument has ceased.

Ryan's Field

A Ferris wheel eclipsed the evening sky
and flung its shadow on my bedroom wall,
I closed my eyes but couldn't sleep, all day
I'd stood on tip-toe at the window watching
the advent of the marvellous trucks piled high
with tents and wooden horses unloading
in Ryan's field, the men hoisting the marquee,
bolting the carousel, making a paradise
of gaudy magic, their silhouettes
labouring in the twilight. In the morning
my mother would take me to the carnival, but that night
I slumbered to the dancing of hammers, dreamt
of wooden horses galloping in Ryan's field.

Danse Macabre

That day the meadow was a sea of breakers;
wind flapped her best sheets on the line,
clothes-pegs in her mouth, Gran
towered above me, helping me
hoist the bunting of wet shirts.

At her funeral the priest's
words echo past me;
for solace I recall a parade
of linens, nylons, cotton, polyester,
reds, greens, gold and purple dancing.

Transformations

Eight centuries of rain
re-carved the gothic stones to rubble;
an offering of rain-water
fills the moss-encrusted font and
as it was in the beginning
vetch and gorse
populate the roofless nave.

And all the faithful?
Gone from the world of light
they lie dreaming
under the rich earth
or are born again
as grasses and wild daisies.

And their celebrant?
He rises this morning as that willow sapling;
his leaves giving praise to the risen sun.

Sonita

That August evening ebbed
over the city's jumble
of roofs and spires. You
were sitting at the open window,
a cigarette lazing
in your hand –
its threads of smoke
untangling slowly
into the air,
as we made small talk,
and the radio,
ignored, babbled to itself
of rush-hour traffic
in the suburbs, on the N7.
But what hurry was on us, the whole
of our lifetimes still before us.

Newly Married

She kneels beside her shadow in the nave:
it's early Mass and she has left her husband
sleeping in their house. Two rows behind her
I imagine her brown eyes closed in adoration,
the gold ring on her finger teasing the sun.

Bartók in Carpathia

Each summer you forsake the conservatoire,
your study of Wagner,
for the woodlands of Carpathia, to hop
from village to low thatched village
lugging in your humped knapsack
an Edison Home Phonograph;
then sitting cricket-like
beside the open fires to coax
from shepherds and swinherds
their ancient music; the needle
incising on wax cylinders
notas and folk dances and the chirping voice
of a forester's daughter singing
shy love-songs in her mother's kitchen.

In the deep, insect-singing night you dream
of the concertos you will compose,
a music half-way between
Wagner's *Tristan*
and the grasshopper's agitated love-song.

A Morisco Song

A lute sighs and above the records hiss
a woman's voice cries
into the air an exile's song.
Each night,
back from work, I play this track
and it never fails: the singer grieving
for the lost minarets of Granada,
the scent of oranges in the evening air,
her art turning loss into cadences and trills
a dark rose flowering in the Moroccan sands,
the last notes slip from the lutanist's hand.

Hanratty's House

Desolate for years,
its walls ache
for the touch of hands,

cattle shelter behind its gable
and an ash tree
stretches its limbs

through the open doorway
of what was once
the tidiest cottage in the parish.

Half a century earlier
the stone-flagged kitchen
overflowed with talk and music:

Billy Maher squeezing a tune
from a concertina,
and the neighbours gathering in

to see Michael off,
Hanrattys' only son,
comforting his mother with how

he'd be back in no time,
talking like a Yank,
his pockets stuffed with dollars.

On The Sideline

They're calling names
in the primary school-yard,
Jimmy and Brendan
naming their sides.

The class divides evenly
into a referee, two teams
and one left over
and that one is Seán.

That one is always Seán,
sitting it out
on the stone wall,
the wind keeping him company.

Lunchtime over, the teams, the referee
and he back in the warm classroom
for Geography and Maths.

Seán, who has by heart,
all the towns of Munster,
on his home turf.

Selkie

The wireless threatens storms: in our farmhouse kitchen
warnings of gales in Malin, Rockall, Irish Sea
spill over an unfinished breakfast.
You tremble and I reassure
telling how, miles inland
our limestone walls and slated barns
frustrate the storm's desire.
But you are thinking of your childhood town,
trawlers at anchor riding the swell,
the ocean coming over the granite pier, and John,
a boy you knew who went to sea,
who will lie tonight
tossed by the ocean's passionate embrace.

After Hokusai

Ambushed by a gust of wind,
      the scholar
is lost in a swirl of clothing:
      straw hat
cartwheels across the sky,
      his sheaf of poems
are loosed into the air.

The inquisitive storm
      flutters the papers
reading every page at once –
the scholar's thirty-seven erudite haiku
      scatter across
      the rice-fields,
      dismissed
      by the tempest's howling rhapsody.

And only Fuji,
its sacred outline misting in the distance,
unmoved by either the scholar or the storm.

* *Katsushika Hokusai (1760-1849), Japanese woodblock
  artist*

The Willow Tree

staggered above me, shaking its many arms
at the laughing sky. Sometimes
its green cloak stole the sun, or
its winter branches clawed the stars
and trapped the half-moon in its web.

And then one day I came home
to find it gone: all its limbs
broken on the grass, gnarled roots
raised up to the air, and where
it had stood – the racing sky.

Eumaeus' Hut

...The inventive Odysseus launched into his story...

– The Odyssey, book XIV.

A storm had levelled the power-lines and we sat
(my father, my great-uncle and myself)
in the candlelit kitchen, a cup
of tea gone tepid in my hands,
but I was lapping up every drop
of their talk. My father mentioned the storm
of 1903. The older man then spoke
of how that afternoon the heavens darkened;
the air's unearthly chill, the wind
screeching with the fury of a Siren.
And suddenly I was a shepherd-boy
in the crackling fire-light of Eumaeus' hut,
listening to Odysseus tell how his men
unlaced the straps that tied the Bag of Winds
and a close-by pine tree creaked in the gale,
and storm-waves thundered in the bay.

Expulsion from Paradise

The bronze gates of Eden slammed against them,
they flee into humanity's first night:
Adam weeps, cowering in shame, but Eve

shivers with joy under the unmapped stars
her mind pregnant with hope as if she knew
of their ordained adventure

the islands and oceans they will name
the making of cities and mythologies,
     and tomorrow
          the first day of history.

Apples in Winter

for Pádraig O'Caoimh, master fiddler of Sliabh Lúachra

Streetlamps against an October night;
the town glistens like a galaxy.
Hallowe'en. Children masked as demons haunt
the leafy avenues. Awaiting them
I kill time with music. The tape unwinding
in the cassette-deck – O'Caoimh, his slurred violin
invokes the wind-whipped fields, a keening storm,
the rattling dance of rain on out-house roofs.

And you Pádraig – ten years dead – alive now
in this music in this room. At the dark
corner of my eye your shadow bows
Apples in Winter, flooding the suburb
with a pagan dance. Shattered
when the doorbell brings unfamiliar children
tricked out as ghosts,
their arms brimming with apples.

Dying World

A tiny life
tapping at the glass
this last wasp
trapped indoors
on the wrong side of our window
scales the invisible pane
unseen wall preventing her flight
until my hand
unlatches the casement
releases her

September 2nd 1939

The dawn invades your curtained room. Outside
a Brussels street-tram hums, a paper-boy
shouts the sudden news of Danzig bombed,
Daladier's reply. You stretch awake,
recall yesterday's events; exchanging vows
before the country priest, the wedding guests
manoeuvring on the dancefloor,
your anxious night of love in this small hotel.

Warsaw smoulders. But that
is someone else's grief, in your brief
seclusion you lie ecstatically content.
Dawn strides towards morning,
a street-tram whines into the distance,
your husband's body slumbers at your side.